MORE
Mind-Bending
Lateral Thinking Puzzles
(Volume II)

Lagoon Books, London

Series Editor: Simon Melhuish
Puzzle Compilation: Nick Hoare
Design & Illustration: Linley Clode
Editors: Hannah Robson and Simon Melhuish

Published by:
LAGOON BOOKS
PO BOX 311, KT2 5QW, UK

ISBN 1 89971 219 4
©LAGOON BOOKS 1996. Lagoon Books is a trade mark
of Lagoon Trading Company Limited.
All rights reserved.

Printed in Singapore.

MORE

MIND-BENDING

LATERAL THINKING

PUZZLES

(VOLUME II)

OTHER TITLES AVAILABLE FROM LAGOON BOOKS:

<u>MIND BENDING PUZZLE BOOKS</u>

MIND-BENDING LATERAL THINKING PUZZLES	(ISBN 1899712062)
MIND-BENDING CONUNDRUMS & PUZZLES	(ISBN 1899712038)
MIND-BENDING CLASSIC LOGIC PUZZLES	(ISBN 1899712186)
MIND-BENDING CLASSIC WORD PUZZLES	(ISBN 1899712054)
MIND-BENDING CROSSWORD PUZZLES	(ISBN 1899712399)

FANTASTIC OPTICAL ILLUSIONS & PUZZLES	(ISBN 1899712402)
WHERE IN THE WORLD AM I? -	(ISBN 1899712410)
MYSTERY GEOGRAPHY PUZZLES	
AFTER DINNER GAMES	(ISBN 1899712429)
MIND-BOGGLERS	(ISBN 1899712445)
PUB TRIVIA QUIZ	(ISBN 189971250X)
60 SECOND MURDER PUZZLES	(ISBN 1899712453)

<u>MYSTERY PUZZLE BOOKS</u>

DEATH AFTER DINNER	(ISBN 1899712461)
MURDER ON THE RIVIERA EXPRESS	(ISBN 189971247X)
MURDER IN MANHATTAN	(ISBN 1899712488)
MURDER AT THRIPPLETON HALL	(ISBN 1899712496)

50 OF THE FINEST DRINKING GAMES	(ISBN 1899712178)
LATERAL DRINKING PUZZLES	(ISBN 1899712208)
TRIVIA ON TAP - BAR ROOM BANALITY	(ISBN 1899712216)
LAUGHS ON DRAUGHT - PUB JOKE BOOK	(ISBN 1899712224)

Books can be ordered from bookshops by quoting the above ISBN numbers.
Some titles may not be available in all countries. All titles are available in the UK.

Lagoon Books has brought together yet more brain-twisting lateral thinking puzzles, giving the reader another refreshingly wide range of challenges, some requiring only a small leap of perception, others deep and detailed thought. All the books in the Mind-Bending range share an eye-catching and distinctive visual style that presents each problem in an appealing and intriguing way. Do not, however, be deceived; what is easy on the eye is not necessarily easy on the mind!

What do you put on the table, cut and then pass around, but would never actually eat?

Two miners were sitting on a bench. One miner was the other one's son, but the other one was not his father. Why?

A prisoner was made to carry a heavy sandbag from one side of the compound to the other. When he got to the other side, he had to take it back again. This went on, hour after hour, day after day, until the prisoner realised that he could put something in the bag that would make it lighter. What was it?

EGG, FISH, TABLE, FOUNDATION, BET. Which is the odd one out?

EGG

FISH

FOUNDATION

TABLE

BET

I have two money boxes of exactly the same size, and two types of coin. The small coins are solid gold and worth $10. The larger coins are exactly twice the size, contain twice the amount of gold, and are worth $20. If I fill one money box with small coins and one with large, which will contain the greatest value when full?

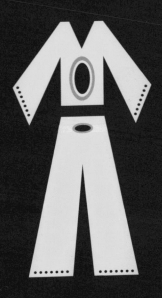

My kind old aunt collects buttons, but even in an emergency she wouldn't let you sew any of them onto a garment. Why not?

I'm inside, halfway up a building that has no windows or balconies, yet I've got an incredible view of the city around me. What sort of building am I in?

Mr and Mrs Brown have got four daughters, who have each got a husband, two brothers and two sons. Can all the Browns fit into a 4 seater car?

My _____ is _____ than my wallet.
Which one word can fill both gaps?

The United manager was talking to his team after the match, when he pointed at Bryan Johnson, who was one of the laziest, most inept players on the pitch, and said, "If only we had five players like him." Has he gone mad?

How many times does the digit 3 appear between 1 and 50?

I had to meet an Australian, an American and a South African at the airport. One of them was called Bruce, and I identified him immediately, despite never having met any of them before. How?

What can explode slowly, with no smoke or flame?

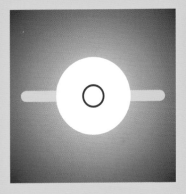

Look at the diagram above. What is it?

Why is Ireland different from Scotland, England, Wales and France?

Sheriff Tom Jones rode into town on Friday, stayed three nights and left early Sunday morning. Explain.

I bumped into my long-lost uncle from Alaska in the street. I'd never met him, seen his picture or heard him described, yet I recognised him immediately. How?

How many times can you subtract 3 from 39?

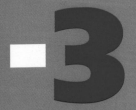

Correct or incorrect? The last woman to be hung in the UK was Ruth Ellis, who shot her love.

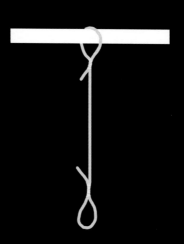

I went to France with something that stopped before we got to the airport. Despite this, it was still with me when I returned. What is it?

What object can you cut clean through, and be left with one object with two ends?

When the family jewels were stolen from inside a vat of vinegar and oil, my brother immediately suspected my sister's widow, but I knew this was wrong. How?

A man walks into a well-lit room and flicks the switch. The lights flicker, and the man leaves, contented. Why?

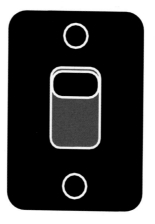

I've got ten or more daughters. I've got less than ten daughters. I've got at least one daughter. If only one of these statements is true, how many daughters have I got?

A father has three daughters who were all born on the 3rd May, 1968. They are not however, triplets. Explain.

What happened in Paris on June 31st 1945?

1945

A prisoner survived ten weeks in a cell without water, and with a 20cm thick steel door between him and a fresh water well in the next cell. How?

When you're looking for something, you always seem to find it in the last place you thought of looking. There is a proven explanation of this. What is it?

100S549A3

100F4E621T

0028Y2167

What famous expression is this?
100S549A3100F4E621T0028Y2167

How many Queens have been crowned in England since 1831?

What can move and be still at the same time?

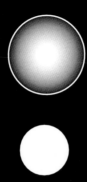

A sphere's got three, a circle's got two, but a point hasn't got any. What?

" I cycled west from London to Bristol. Stopping twice for a rest, I finished the journey in record time, helped along by a gusting west wind." What is wrong with this?

A woman has three daughters who in turn, each have three daughters. If they all get together in one room, how many pairs of sisters are present?

My birthday is January 5th, but I always celebrate it in the summer. Who am I?

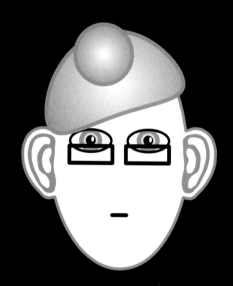

TRUE? FALSE?

Which is true? One statement here is false? Two statements here are false? Three statements here are false?

I bet you that if you stand on one end of my tie, and I stand on the other, you will not be able to touch me. How?

I'm on Earth, but I'm not in a time zone, nor am I between two time zones. Where am I?

*A*t 8:34 precisely, on the day that President Nixon resigned, he looked out of a south facing White House window but couldn't see the top of the Empire State Building. Why not?

What is impossible to hold for half an hour, yet weighs virtually nothing?

*A*t a family reunion one man went up to another. "Father!" "Grandad?" replied the other. Neither was mistaken. Explain.

In a balloon, stationary off the coast of Ireland, I dropped two wine bottles off the side. If one was full and the other empty, which hit the ground first?

They can be made, laid down, bent and broken, although it's difficult to touch them. What are they?

WHAT

ARE

THEY?

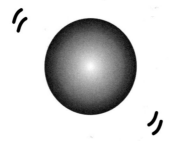

A professional footballer bet me that he could kick a ball a certain distance, have it stop, and then come back to him, without anything else touching it. He won the bet. How?

If you are walking forwards, but travelling back-
wards, and the only motion is being provided by you
(not on a train, in a river etc.), where are you?

HOROBOD is a clue to the identity of a famous historical figure. Who is it?

A woman has three daughters who in turn, each have three daughters. If they all get together in one room, how many pairs of grandmothers and granddaughters are there?

What mathematical symbol can you put between 2 and 3 to make a number greater than 2, but less than 3?

Which English word do Australians always pronounce incorrectly?

How can I not sleep for 10 days and not be tired?

I was told by a magician to repeat "lemon" three times, so I said "Lemon, lemon, lemon", whereupon he angrily said "Didn't you hear what I said?". What should I have said?

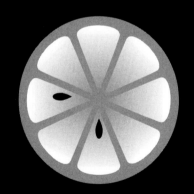

*A*ntonio was a virtuoso musician who had never touched an instrument or written a note of music in his life. Explain.

A prisoner is kept on 50 grains of rice and a bowl of water a day. Despite getting progressively weaker he manages to pull the bars from his window and escape after a year. How?

L ook at the diagram below. What is it?

My grandmother is one of the sweetest, politest, and most generous people I know, so imagine my surprise when I found a book in her house called "Go to Hell". On closer inspection I realised my error. Explain.

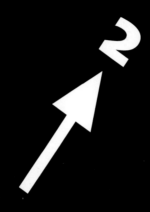

If a clock takes 2 seconds to strike 2 o'clock, how long will it take to strike 3 o'clock?

How many string quartets are there in a dozen?

A victorious football team return home as champions of Europe. Their 1km long entourage moves at a rate of 1km/hour through the crowded streets. How long will it take to pass completely through the 1km long main square?

I have 25 hankies, equally divided into five different colours. If I were blindfolded, how many would I have to pick out to be sure of having one of each colour?

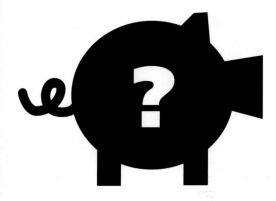

In a pig sty, each of the sows can see an equal number of sows and male pigs, but each male pig sees twice as many sows as male pigs. How many pigs are there in total?

At midnight it is raining hard. How probable is it that it will be sunny in 72 hours time?

I'm in a tent, but it offers me no protection from the wind, rain or snow, yet I don't want to leave it. Why?

What holds water, but is full of holes?

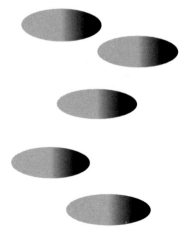

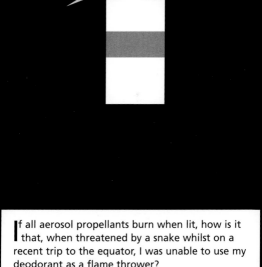

If all aerosol propellants burn when lit, how is it that, when threatened by a snake whilst on a recent trip to the equator, I was unable to use my deodorant as a flame thrower?

If four boys can pick four apples in four minutes, how many boys would be able to pick 100 apples in 100 minutes?

I have two buckets of the same size. If I fill one with small pebbles, and one with large stones, which bucket will be heaviest?

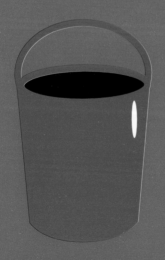

Dave looked under a table and saw a hand, completely detached from an arm. He looked over at Alan, and although all his fingers and thumbs were in place, and his hands were attached to his arms, he knew the hand beneath the table must be his. He stood up and punched him. Why?

*A*s I left the reptile house at the zoo I felt something
move in my pocket. I put my hand in, and
discovered something with no legs and several teeth.
Once I'd got over my initial surprise and had identified
it correctly, I was happy to leave it there undisturbed.
What was it?

What gets wetter as it dries?

Can you guess the next letter in this series?
C Y G T N L I T . . . ?

C Y G T N L I T . . . ?

Racing driver Ramon Ricard had a terrible accident at Daytona leaving him in hospital for 6 months. Surprisingly, he never once considered giving up racing. Why not?

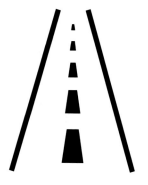

HOW MANY

CHILDREN

ARE THERE?

In a certain family, each girl has as many sisters as brothers but each boy has twice as many sisters as brothers. How many children are there?

I can stick a pin into a balloon without it making a noise or releasing any air. How?

They are a dozen-strong gang, laden with jewels, weapons, internal organs and gardening equipment. Some of them are visually impaired, yet they have been sighted all over the place. Who or what are they?

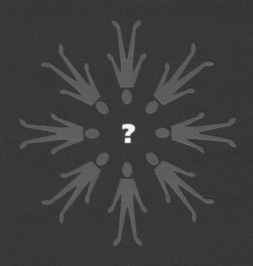

Dave married two women, without divorcing either of them, and with neither woman divorcing him, committing bigamy or dying. Explain.

Even though I have only a 25, a 10 and three 5 cent coins, I can still make 30 cents with two coins even though one of them is not the 25 cent coin. How?

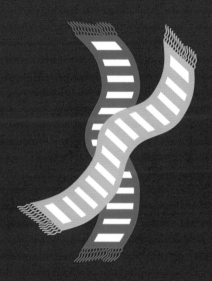

My favourite team have won seven times this season, but they haven't scored a goal. Explain.

What do you break by saying its name?

I am standing on a bare stone floor, and I am holding a very fragile, very brittle porcelain cup. I am certain, however, that I can drop the cup through more than a metre without it breaking. How?

It was 3:30pm, and sinister magician Umbro the Unnatural was standing in the middle of a park. There were no trees around him, and not a cloud in the sky, yet he cast no shadow. How did he do this?

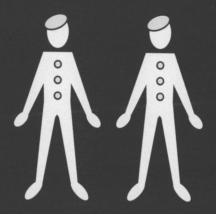

What's the smallest number of people you need to assemble two uncles and two nephews in the same place?

If I walked without an umbrella or a raincoat or a hat across a treeless plain for an hour, how did I avoid getting wet?

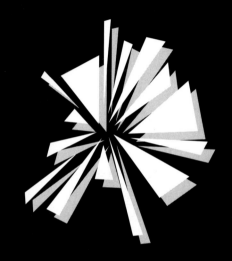

A man is killed by a pane of glass. The glass didn't fall on him, and it wasn't broken before it killed him. So how did he die?

I can tie a knot in a piece of string without letting go of either of the ends. How?

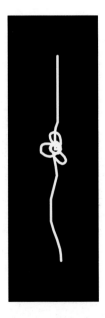

solutions

Page 6
A deck of cards.

Page 7
She was his mother.

Page 8
A hole.

Page 9
You can't lay a fish.

Page 10
Despite the difference in size, you will get the same value of coins into each money box.

Page 11
She collects buttons from radios, televisions and lifts.

Page 12
A multi-storey car park.

Page 13
Yes. There are only four of them; Mr and Mrs Brown and their two sons. The other 16 have married names.

Page 14
LIGHTER

Page 15
No. United have played a disastrous game, and they would have fared better if only five of the players were as incompetent as Johnson, not all eleven of them.

Page 16
15 times: 3, 13, 23, 30, 31, 32, 33 (two 3s), 34, 35, 36, 37, 38, 39, 43.

Page 17
The other two were called Lucy and Mary.

Page 18
A population.

Page 19
A bird's-eye view of a man on a bicycle wearing a sombrero.

Page 20
It's got three vowels.

Page 21
Friday is the name of his horse.

Page 22
He is my dad's identical twin.

Page 23
Once. After that you're subtracting 3 from 36, and so on.

Page 24
Incorrect. People are hanged, not hung.

Page 25
A watch.

Page 26
Any sort of loop.

Page 27
My sister can't have a widow.

Page 28
He is an executioner, and came in to test the electric chair, which always makes the lights flicker.

Page 29
None. If "I've got at least one daughter" is true, then "I've got ten or more daughters" can also be true, and vice versa. "I've got less than ten daughters" can be true by itself, but only if I have no daughters.

Page 30
They are three of four quads.

Page 31
Absolutely nothing. June has only got 30 days.

Page 32
The door wasn't locked.

Page 33
It's always the last place because, once you've found it, you stop looking.

Page 34
SAFETY in numbers.

Page 35
None. Both Victoria and Elizabeth II were princesses when they were crowned.

Page 36
A carton of orange juice.

Page 37
Dimensions. A point is a place. It has no form.

Page 38
A west wind would slow you down if you were cycling to the west, as it blows from the west.

Page 39
12.

Page 40
Someone who lives in the southern hemisphere.

Page 41
Two statements here
are false.

Page 42
If I thread my tie under a
door, we wouldn't be able to
touch each other.

Page 43
At one of the poles.

Page 44
Because the White House is
in Washington and the
Empire State in New York.

Page 45
Your breath.

Page 46
The grandson was a priest.

Page 47
Neither hit the ground. I was
over the sea.

Page 48
Rules.

Page 49
He kicked it straight up in
the air.

Page 50
On a log, a large ball, or
any spherical or cylindrical
object.

Page 51
Robin Hood. ROB in HOOD
HO(ROB)OD.

Page 52
There are 9.

Page 53
A decimal point.

Page 54
Incorrectly.

Page 55
By sleeping at night.

Page 56
"Lemon, lemon, lemon,
lemon." If he'd told me to
repeat "lemon" once, I
should have said it twice.

Page 57
He was a singer.

Page 58
Every day he would save
and dry a couple of grains
of rice, put them in the
cracks around the bars and
pour some water on them.
Gradually the swelling
increased the size of
the cracks and loosened
the bars.

Page 59

A Trombonist in a portable toilet!

Page 60

It was the sixth volume of an encyclopedia.

Page 61

4 seconds. If the time between the clapper striking the bell for the first peal and the second peal is 2 seconds, then it will be a further two seconds before it strikes for the third peal.

Page 62

12.

Page 63

Two hours. The front of the procession will take an hour, and will be leaving the square just as the tail-end enters it.

Page 64

21.

Page 65

Four sows and three male pigs.

Page 66

72 hours later it will be midnight.

Page 67

I'm in an oxygen tent.

Page 68

A sponge.

Page 69

I use roll-on deodorant.

Page 70

Four. As a team, they can, on average, pick one a minute.

Page 71

They will both weigh the same – surprisingly, no matter what the size of the stones the proportion of stone to air space remains the same.

Page 72

They were playing cards. The "extra hand" was a set of duplicate cards, proving that Alan was cheating.

Page 73

A comb I hadn't seen in a while.

Page 74

A towel.

Page 75

S. They are the first letters

of each of the words of
the question.

Page 76
Because he fell down
some stairs.

Page 77
Three boys and four girls.

Page 78
The balloon isn't inflated.

Page 79
A pack of cards.

Page 80
Dave is a priest who
conducted two weddings.

Page 81
By using a 25 and a 5 cent
coin. Although one of them
is not the 25 cents, the other
one is.

Page 82
It is a cricket team.

Page 83
Silence.

Page 84
If I hold the cup 2 metres off
the ground, it will fall 1.99m

without breaking. The final
0.01m will, however, cause it
to shatter into tiny pieces.

Page 85
It was a winter's afternoon
in Scotland and it was
already dark.

Page 86
Two. If two men marry
each other's mothers, they
automatically become
half-brothers. So, if they
have one son each, then
the other one's son is
automatically nephew
and uncle!

Page 87
It wasn't raining.

Page 88
He fell through it from a
great height, rather than it
falling on him.

Page 89
By picking up the string with
my arms folded, and then
unfolding them.

We are indebted to a number of fellow puzzlers and thinkers
who have provided us with inspiration for this book, in particular Dr. Edward
de Bono, Martin Gardner, Boris A. Kordemsky, Victor Serebriakoff, Paul
Sloane, & Trevor Truran.

FURTHER READING:

MIND-BENDING LATERAL THINKING PUZZLES (VOL I) (Lagoon Books 1995)

LATERAL DRINKING PUZZLES: A Cocktail of Conundrums for Connoisseurs
(Lagoon Books 1996)

AHA! INSIGHT by Martin Gardner (W H Freeman 1978)

CHALLENGING LATERAL THINKING PUZZLERS by Paul Sloane and Des MacHale
(Sterling Publishing 1992)

LATERAL THINKING PUZZLES by Paul Sloane (Sterling Publishing 1991)

MASTERFUL MINDBENDERS by Trevor Truran (Octopus Books 1984)

MIND OPENERS FOR MANAGERS by John O'Keefe (Thorsons 1994)

MINDBENDERS LOGIC GAMES by Norman Barrett (Kingfisher Books 1992)